Escaping the Poverty Cycle

CW00420451

Contents

Chapters

1. The family and Support network
   Definition
   Reasons for continued poverty
   Family structure

2. Education is the key to success?
   Education starts at home
   Education on finances

3. Inheritance and what we leave behind
   Benefiting the future generations
   Tax to be considered

4. Respect towards our own culture
   Long term focus rather than short
   Living beyond our means

5. Our view of ourselves
   What shapes our view?
   Learn the business side of whatever you do

6. Our sense of worth
   Where our worth derives from?
   Celebrity influence over heritage

7. The role of Media power
   Images given
   Portrayal of Black people

8. The effects of slavery
   Slavery
   Colonialism
   The Civil Rights Movement
   Apartheid
   Summary

9. Appropriation of culture
   Definition
   What occurs today?

10. Investing in knowledge
    Reading is important
    Is age a factor?

11. Influential black financial figures
    Black businesses
    Black Wall Street

12. The benefits of a healthy lifestyle
    The mental element
    Physical exercise
    Eating right

13. The tax system – who benefits?
    Corporate tax
    Marginal tax

14. Your aim in life
    Who do we look to?
    An Action plan

15. Time is an investment
    Interaction between family and friends
    Positive talk

Sources

Synopsis

For anyone from a working class background or anyone just interested in how they can better themselves and their families' future this book opens up a few simple ideas in an understandable way. Many of us have the ideas but may not know the best way of going about implementing them or just need a straightforward guide.

Presented by a working class man who understands issues both in the present and past and is trying to offer simple solutions to try or consider.

This is not a ten step program telling you how rich you can be by simply following instructions from a rich author. This was a great pleasure for me to write, learn and get insight into subjects from other people's perspective and I hope you enjoy reading it.

Disclaimer

This book does not guarantee anything but it can give a better outlook on life and lead to a better future for the next generation. We can individually make the change and instil these values in our children.

Allot of people may have this knowledge and think it is an insult to address these issues directly towards black families and the working class, but are the majority of us working towards better goals for our next generation. It is not a generalization or negative review of our culture/heritage but seeks to uplift and offer ideas. As a young black male I find there is a lack of books that teach black history and this is rarely in the curriculum so I have included a brief section here to give a perspective on how our race is behind in the financial world.

This is by no means financial advice or guaranteed solutions by all means legal advice should always be sought before making financial investments. This book is constructive feedback from discussions with black individuals and working class families on what they believe needs addressing.

Acknowledgements

Thank you to God without whom I would not have the knowledge to have completed this book or have any ideas.

This book is dedicated to my first born who may be born by the time it is released.
To my wife for being so supportive and pushing me to do better.
And of course my mother and dad without whom I could not be here. To my older brother Mark, younger sister Natalie and younger brother Gavin.

Escaping the poverty cycle

Aim of this book

This book focuses on trying to help people realise the economic troubles that may have them and their future generation not working together and believing the myths we are taught from a young age. This does not cover all aspects on how we can work together to uplift one another the black race and working class, it is just a start to be taken further by ourselves with investment of our time on ourselves and family.

The target audience is not aimed only at black families or working class it is for any race, class, gender or religion written by a black man (myself) to address issues I have seen throughout my life and by no means covers all topics and problems faced in our society.

Chapter One

The Family and Support network

Summary

There are things we do not realise when we are young that influence our thinking and it is these factors that are discussed and addressed. By addressing these issues it enables people to pin point factors that may have influenced their decisions and to help them consider alternative views.

I always perceived being a homeowner as being in a big debt for a long period of time but this is not necessarily the entire fact it can also be viewed as an investment if not for yourself than for your next generation so they inherit a home when you are older.

There is also the option of taking money out once you have put in a reasonable amount but this obviously has to be paid back. In today's market, prices are going up so your investment today will be worth more in the future there is also the possibility of a decline in the market but like with shares a mortgage is an investment to view over time that gives options.

Introduction

Definition

Let us start with a brief definition of what the Poverty cycle means:

Factors or events by which poverty is likely to continue unless there is outside intervention. Typically defined as three generations of an impoverished family with no means of possessing or transferring intellectual, social and cultural capital to change the circumstance.

There are other sub categories to consider such as financial capital, education and connections.

Financial capital can be used to invest in shares, start a business, secure a car/ mortgage or earn interest off.

The right education not necessarily a formal school based one can open doors to high paid skilled jobs or give a grounding in how to run a business. Connections allow people to associate with people in high places that may be able to give great work experience, be used as a reference or provide a good job.

We cannot always blame external factors we have to look internally as well and ask how hard we are prepared to work to achieve something or do we just want an easy life free from work?

Reasons for continued poverty

Some reasons for continued poverty:

-Low productivity
-Low salary
-Poor infrastructure and governance
-Business failure
-Ignorance lack of skills in technology
-Unhealthy
-Inability to access resources such as information from technology or libraries
-No further education
-Lack of interaction with people with knowledge

Considering some of the bullet points above:

Low productivity
Many including myself just do "my job" which means they are only going to do their designated tasks for the day but anything extra to help others in the same area of work or team may be considered. People have to understand the people who get promotions are those doing extra but not trying to draw attention to the fact they are helping they are just genuinely helpful and useful and thus are seen as potential because they do more than is required. I myself have failed many times to do extra but this is just not in everyone. Whilst working as a temp I was in a team of ten preparing bundles for a court trial and one individual seemed to be working harder than anyone else and asking if he could do anything else. When the temp role finished I went to other jobs but when I came back to the same company as a temp this individual was now giving instructions to a team that included an individual that I went to university with and continued to be working hard but now was permanent and well paid and a team leader.

Low salary
With a low salary it is hard to get loans, a mortgage or a car and thus can inhibit what you can do in terms of travelling to further areas for work or enabling you to be places faster. With a low salary you may also be deemed unable to afford a mortgage or repay a loan.

Business failure
If people have tried and failed at business it is hard to attempt it again and get the full backing of a bank with a business loan if you do not have enough money yourself to invest or show a well presented business plan.

Ignorance or lack of skills in technology
Some refuse to apply for jobs thinking they would not get them but often you do not go into a job knowing how to do everything you have to learn. Sometimes we believe we cannot learn and understand modern technology because it is not part of our generation and what we grew up with but technology is often designed to be easy to use and understand thus appealing to more people.

Unhealthy
Health factors can limit availability for work or the types of work people will be considered for.

Inability to access resources such as information from technology or libraries
Many of a certain generation have not grown up with computer skills and may find it difficult to learn how to use a computer or are reluctant to thus inhibiting the amount of work they can be considered for or how far they can advance in a job.

Lack of interaction with people with knowledge
If people are limited to their interactions with people from higher paid jobs then there is a limit placed on a person's ability to understand that role or think about doing that profession. However they can view it in the media and this may seem even more distant from their ability since it is not something they see in the real world but on TV or in the paper.

The question has to be asked, is there a mismatch in people's skills and the jobs available? There are some highly skilled individuals every year coming from universities and straight from school but their skills are not being made use of due to the economic times that we have been living in. I believe myself to be one of these individuals with a degree and masters and I still do not obtain jobs that reflect the pay or skills I have studied.
People have to settle for jobs that are not related to what they studied for or just what is available. Gone are the days where you could leave a job that was not suitable and find another one relatively easy.

Do we have a pre exposed nature/culture with beliefs that there is a system or reasons for our lack? Many believe there is a system where the world is run by very few extremely rich individuals that run corporations that have control over our media and government and thus us. This is often referred to as the elite theory.

Time is treated differently by different classes of people it is argued that the poor do not plan ahead but live in the moment and this stops them from saving money that could help their children escape poverty it is also argued an inherited helplessness is learnt from parents. This leads to people spending money as soon as they get it often on cigarettes or alcohol. It is argued by many there are feelings amongst the poor of dependency vulnerability this could be influenced by our benefits system that in some circumstances makes it more profitable to be on benefits than work.

Family structure

Studies have looked at the household structure and whether single parent families impact a child and their future wealth. It would make sense that a family with a mum and dad would be able to afford more and therefore provide more for a child in certain aspects possibly allowing a child to have an easier time to focus on their future with less worries financially and with more support emotionally on offer from two rather than one guide.

Looking at the father's' role and support from others, children who grow up without fathers can often feel abandonment and neglect. When boys grow up without a father figure they can either totally respect the woman (mother) that raised them or women (aunt and grandma) or have the reverse happen and not have an appreciation for women. This lack of respect towards women can lead to men making babies without looking after them with emotional support, physical or financial. This can lead to women relying on benefits to raise a child and thus not be in a position to pursue future wealth for a child or themselves.

When women have to make a choice between work and benefits this often maintains the cycle of poverty with less of a demand for a child's further education.

Some families have it instilled in them to stay together in a house so they can pay the rent more easily than if they paid it alone and allow the children to save until they can move out whilst contributing towards bills. Having more than two kids can be costly but is also like a future investment, I am not trying to start a baby boom or saying to have kids to be financially better off but I am advocating working with people that you can trust and that have your best interest which is usually immediate family.

Most of us usually either do not stay together long as a family because:

- A child leaves home seeking independence
- Marriage dissolves
- We do not have as many kids
- have rifts that mean we cannot work together;

Growing up I was not raised in a home that was paid for under a mortgage I grew up in a council property which is perfectly fine but it was a spacious three bedroom property if my parent had a mortgage on it, it would be worth allot or we could have sold and bought something just as good.

In the past people worked together to give their children a better start so they are ahead by passing on a family business (corner shop, market stall) etc.

Currently forecasts are saying current generations are worse off than their parents due to a lack in wage growth and increases in every other area that requires money (rent, food, oil prices).
Ask yourselves now do you have any relatives that you can trust to invest with you? To obtain a mortgage to buy a place to share (live with) until the mortgage is paid off so you have a family home. Or get a mortgage so you can develop a place with new features and sell when the property increases in value.

If the answer is no, Why is this? Why do we not have family we can trust? Most of us grow up trusting our friends more rather than our own blood. When did it become a good thing to be untrustworthy when it comes to money and not want to work together to make a better future for more than just ourselves.

If a child growing up has a family home debt free they can work on getting another rather than starting from nothing or try to spend their money on investments. If they can acquire another home there is rental income to be made so even if unemployed there is the security of an income but you should insure if possible this is enough to cover the mortgage you currently have. But in an ideal scenario your current mortgage is being paid for by your rental income and you are working so you have all of your salary to spend rather than forty per cent or more of your salary going towards rent or a mortgage.

There are allot of people that are having to move out of flats or houses that have been in their family for years because they thought it is with the council it will always be affordable or it is a guaranteed home for life but that is not the case at least if you have a mortgage you can sell and make money and move on but this does not even have to be an option, as long as you can afford the mortgage than you can stay in your home with literally no problem. Unless some sort of construction (highway) is deemed necessary or the property is dangerous to yourself or others the government should not require the sale of your house/flat. And this is how it should be no one can tell you that you have to move to a different area because you have too many rooms or they are knocking down the flats to build something more expensive so you cannot afford it and they can bring rich people into the area. The word used to describe the above few paragraphs is gentrification where an area that is considered relatively poor is invested in for the purpose of bringing in middle class people and reallocating poorer people.

Do we know what makes a property increase in value? Below are some ideas:

-new shops in the area (supermarket) means convenience for people nearby having to travel less to get goods
-offices being built nearby means jobs and an increase in money spent in the area
-a new bath such as heated tiles, heated towel rail a shower adds value.
-laminate flooring is considered cleaner and is more acceptable to a new tenant than carpet that has been used by a previous owner.
-a converted loft provides extra storage space or can be converted into a room.

We do not save money to pass on in accounts like ISA's. An ISA allows you to save money tax free for a year but there are limits on how much you can save within the year and the interest rate is usually higher within your first year of saving in comparison with an ordinary current account. To withdraw money usually takes longer but the whole idea is to save.

Debt is never helpful and should be avoided or paid off as soon as it can be.

Summary

This chapter looks at the common perception of education equalling success and the pride of families always wanting to show their kids have achieved something by being able to say they have passed or done well in an exam to have a qualification they believe will get them a good job, but this is not always the case.

Introduction

I have often found that sometimes when I wanted a simple job to earn extra such as shop work due to my degree and master's employers were often thinking I was overqualified and would not stay long within the position. For those thinking they can leave their education out of a CV it does become a problem when you have an interview and have to explain certain periods of your life without saying you were studying.

We are taught from young to get the best education we can to get a good job work hard get a house car and your life will be happy and that is about it but for some reason in black and working class families these houses or finances rarely seem to be passed on to children debt free or for them to get a good start in life. The question is asked why that is.

A state education is not a bad thing but it does place a child in debt whereas if they went to work straight away they might be in a better position or have experience to progress higher in a job. Unless there is a specific area that your child's education will always prove valuable or useful (dentistry, doctor) then it has to be looked at in the long term whether it is economically viable.

Education starts at home

Education is best taught from a young age because that is when the brain is best adapted to learn and retain information. We can all add skills to our children such as mathematical skills, languages, musical skills to help them in the future and make learning other transferable skills easier to pick up. Education should always start from home it is not something we should rely on a TV or a school to do because often there are bad influences or habits that can be learnt or just a rigid structure of memorising rather than learning.

Education on finances

Why are we not taught things that enable us to operate independently as our own boss rather than work for others? Instead of building ourselves or community by running a business we are making another man/company rich and often not rewarded well enough for this. As I am writing this I am in work early the irony but am about to start working soon.

We could learn that shares don't have to be complicated there are many companies that will manage shares for you at a reasonable cost. When you invest with them they are not putting all your money into one share they invest in different areas to ensure if one share suffers a loss the next may increase or at least balance it out this is known as diversification. If we are willing to invest in holidays for £1,000 plus sometimes or cars why not shares to make money rather than have something that devalues.

An education from every family should include how to invest wisely and build a business for ourselves even if there are a few failed attempts that is the only way to learn.

Education is not enough you have to have a few extra qualities one of these is:

-skill to be able to apply what you have learnt in the theory (books and classes) to the practical (physically doing).

Secondly nearly every form of work will need skills in communication and team work to be able to work with people and get along is very important.

Thirdly work ethic is important in how you perform tasks and with the right attitude namely a "can do" attitude. Nobody wants someone that wines every time you ask them to do something.

There are more qualities but lastly allot of employers seek people with work experience or people that have shown a dedication by doing a vacation scheme or worked for free in their area of interest.

The big achievers in life are those who practice lifelong learning this allows them to be open to ideas and adapt with the times, life should not be about complacency.

Chapter Three

Inheritance and what we leave behind

Summary

We can instil from a young age a sense of value and worth in our children and teach them the morals of right and wrong but there is still always the need for guidance for a child at any age until they can stand by themselves and say they can take care of themselves morally, financially and in other ways.

Introduction

Obviously we may inherit looks, good habits/bad but what did you individually inherit from your parents? This does not mean only financially our parents could have instilled a sense of drive to achieve, determination or passion to achieve our goals.

Why as working class or poorer families is life insurance not considered to pass on money and wealth to our kids? Most will say they want to earn the money to pass on to their kids (pride) but how much do you pass on realistically.

We believe our kids will make their own destiny and do better than we did because times have changed but there is no harm in giving them a head start.

Benefiting the future generations

If a family cannot rely on social, intellectual or cultural capital then it makes things really difficult to escape the poverty cycle. Values should be instilled so our children can benefit future generations or society.

Many should ask when they are not here anymore what are they leaving for their children:

-A home/flat to provide rental income or live

-Life insurance can help pay towards funeral costs and help towards investment for the trustees

-ISA can provide tax free saving and a higher interest rate than most accounts

-Shares can fluctuate but provide a steady source of income through dividends

-Car that can be used or sold for convenience;

A CNN report "whites have 12 times the wealth of blacks" shows the financial inequality in America, with many not having a firm wealth building plan.

The three main reasons for the wealth gap are:

1) black people are less likely to be homeowners or participate in retirement accounts

2) earning gap makes it harder to save

3) subsidies to buy homes require a certain income level which black people are less likely to reach;

Tax to be considered

A word of caution for those who may be able to leave a reasonable amount behind and that is inheritance tax. Inheritance tax is paid by a person who inherits property or money from a person who has died. The nil rate band is the amount of money/property value you can pass on without paying inheritance tax for 2016 this is £325,000.

Inheritance in some cultures bestows less upon females and more upon sons' sometimes one reason for this is due to the fact that sons tend to keep the family name whereas women change their name and it may be perceived that by leaving an inheritance to a male that inheritance stays within the family.

Without a will many families will fail to leave behind their wealth to the correct trustee which can also lead to disputes from relatives (probate) leading to the courts making a decision rather than the testator (person who died). A will also ensures a person who you think is responsible can distribute your estate (executive).

Chapter Four

Respect towards our own culture

Summary

What do we respect people for? Is it their ability, wealth, friendship, morals, determination or support? Respect should not be about fighting to protect an area which we do not actually own but these days the youth are quick to turn to violence because of their perceived area which can lead to jail or relocation from that area. All it takes is a hit to the head that makes a person lose conscience and they hit their head on the floor and you are a convicted criminal all to protect a house and flat that you do not technically own.

Introduction

I remember seeing my dad walking around areas with me and sometimes he would just acknowledge another black man with a nod and words like "yes my brother" and that would lead to respect or a positive talk between him and the individual whereas these days the youth look to fight for less.

Long term focus rather than short

If the youth of today had a focus of not just "get that p" meaning to get money but was about what they are trying to achieve in the long term by getting that money I. E- feeding their family, property or investing in their own business rather than to buy trainers or expensive clothes to impress there would be less violence because you're too busy focusing on trying to achieve something (like investing in yourself or your own business) where you try to avoid any conflict that could disrupt your goals and seek peace rather than confrontation.

If we fight each other and cannot help each other we are viewed by others in society as dangerous or a problem which is why our youth are misunderstood offered fewer jobs and can end up in prison.

Living beyond our means

Why as poorer people do we try to live the lifestyles of celebrities without the same salary, it is nice to try and see what it is like but it is not a sustainable lifestyle without the equivalent salary. We all have seen women with £300 bags around their arm and designer clothes but they go home to a rented house/flat and have a car they rent or it is not theirs there is nothing wrong with this if this is your choice to indulge yourself but what about your next generation?

Much of society today see illegal activity as a way to make money fast but fail to look at the consequences or believe it is worth the risk but before this stage is reached all options should be looked into. Often all people can see is the lifestyle around them so they can't get outside influences that would benefit.

I often tell younger family members they need to go on a holiday not one to party or drink but to see there is more to the world a different way of living. Sometimes I land in a country and just feel a sense of peace and a calmer environment with people not rushing around angry or aggressive annoyed by public transport.

Do we respect people like Levi Roots? (Reggae, Reggae sauce) a black business man selling pepper sauces or Jamal Edwards (Sb.tv) owns his own media production through YouTube and his own site.

How much do we know about where we are really from? Firstly from our direct family our mother and our father do we know the history of their country and how this may have shaped them individually and their country. With a brief discussion with them you can find out things you may not be told in books or on TV because it will be an actual account of what took place.

Secondly do we know our ancestors history namely African history, whether people agree or not the oldest fossilised body found was that of an African in Ethiopia and scientists have stated all humans have come from Africa. This should be enough for people to stop forms of racism but often this knowledge is not known or accepted.

Summary

The youth of today look at what they see they can achieve as a job or career or they look at areas they are good in and areas people from similar background to themselves have been successful in which is often music and sports. Music can be lucrative but often for many of us this is not a professional career, the view point is short term and not based on the need for a regular income to sustain you.

Introduction

Our view of ourselves is one that is conscious and subconscious and formed through our social interactions. People often try to compare themselves to others at times either to make themselves feel good because they have an ability someone else does not or make themselves feel bad because someone else possesses a skill they admire but do not yet possess.

What shapes our view?

Our view can be shaped by:

–social roles we see or are part of such as being a mother, our job, being a husband.
-reactions from people that can either be reinforcing a held view of ourselves or implementing a new view with a positive or negative affect.
-comparisons in ability, appearance, personality

Our environment often shapes us in our behaviours when young. If we grow up in an area with high crime, drug use or violence then it is often hard for the youth to not be affected by this. Many often see being a part of a gang as protection so other gangs that have rivalries with their area do not attack them, but often being in a gang can cause violence in retaliation for the actions of members.

Many parents try to dissuade their children from dressing similar to the gangs but it often thought of as a lifestyle or trend so children do not want to stand out as different so conform to a certain degree.

Learn the business side of whatever you do

What the youth could be taught that would give them an advantage is the business side of music or sport which involves marketing yourself well as well as your product, not just make a great song people would want but how am I going to protect my rights to this song (copyright, royalties etc.). Even great athletes or musicians have to be aware of the financial side because many have been caught for avoiding tax but this is a simple matter of understanding that it has to be accounted for and is not always automatically taken from you. There is also money to declare to the tax office such as any work that might be considered extra or overtime that you get paid for, it all should be accounted for because it can mean a different tax code or amount to be paid.

Whatever product you sell even if it is music advertising has to be considered on various platforms such as:

-Facebook
-twitter
-blogger
-YouTube
-sound cloud;

As well as sending the track to producers and networking with others.

Do we view ourselves through our:

-class (working, middle, upper)
-inherited features (weight, height, big lips, straight nose, straight hair)
-religion (a spirit in a vessel) or (one with nature from the universe)
-material possessions (car, house, money)
-the way others view us

We can either have a positive view of ourselves (high self-confidence) which can lead us to try things that may benefit us or a negative self-image (low self –confidence) that can lead to depression.

We can promote a good self-image by spending time with good friends/family and being grateful for the skills we do possess. Our view is constantly changing through external factors and that is to be expected.

If we value people's opinions more than our own we can end up trying to live up to their expectations, this is why social media and the celebrity status that children seek can be dangerous. We see many celebrities doing things just to get attention and people talking about them. The reason for this can be to generate attention and thus income through magazine sales and interviews and other forms of media but it can be a confidence issue.

How you view yourself and portray yourself can affect the way others treat you and as long as you are being you and be positive towards others then no one else can replicate whatever talent or skill you have because only you can do that particular thing in the manor you do. Our view of ourselves is vital because it can not only shape relationships with our family and friends but also that of a potential partner. If we do not view allot of positives in marriage then there will be the view that it is unnecessary. As mentioned in an earlier chapter, children from stable families tend to do better in life due to a support network and better social skills being developed.

Summary

Many of the youth if asked where they are from would mention where they were born and even if you say what about your parents many refuse to acknowledge the truth or do not know but the oldest living fossil found is from Africa thus we are all African.

Introduction

Where our worth derives from?

Our sense of worth can derive from many areas and aspects of our life:

- Parents and family
- Friends
- Media (TV, magazines, celebrities and music)
- What we achieve (education and work)
- How much we earn
- Children
- Where we live (conditions) peaceful, dangerous or rich/poor

Celebrity influence over heritage

Celebrities tend to set a trend for what is popular and what is not, often we see black celebrities that were dark in skin colour using bleaching which influences some kids with dark skin to think that being dark is not attractive or that their hair needs to be straight.

We also see celebrities having plastic surgery to slim, gain a cleavage, Botox, a nose job or face lift making people think if they had enough money they can do what they like to achieve what they conceive as perfect or acceptable.

Our heritage is not embraced but regarded as something to be kept quiet. Many would rather mention what they perceive to be more acceptable their straight hair from their relative from a country that will be viewed more favourably.

Many of the youth seem hypnotised by social media trying to get likes and followers by doing what would be considered either cool or outrageous. Yes there is money to be made from this now by getting adequate advertising on your YouTube page or other form of social media. But how far should people go? there are parents catching their children twerking (sexually provocative/seductive) dancing on social media for attention. We do have to think more about the effects on our family and in the working world if we are to be known for these particular actions. Many employers look on social networks to see what an individual is like before hiring them and if you have pictures of yourself getting drunk all the time it is not going to help, unless the employer enjoys that lifestyle themselves.

There has been growth in self-employed contractors although there are less work based benefits such as sick pay, holiday pay and annual leave. There is flexibility as a self-employed contractor to gain work experience, skills or be flexible in the area you work.

Many although unemployed might refuse work believing it is beneath them or they have too much experience to do the job but any form of income that is honestly earned can help and is better than being unemployed. Whilst employed you are active socially and physically and can still apply for the job you want.

However with only limited roles shown to us through media or our environment (family and friends) this leads to limited options.

In the end our self-esteem is what is going to lead us to make positive options for ourselves because we believe in ourselves and have confidence in our abilities.

Summary

What we listen to and see influences us whether we are aware of it or not. Allot of people love the rhythm/beat of a song before they know the words and they often sing the catchy part of the song as long as it is repetitive.
Do the media help the situation? Promoting things with celebrity stories and gossip.
When I mention media that encompasses (TV, film, music and newspapers).

Introduction

The most recent event the Oscars showed a lack of diversity being highlighted by black actors namely (Jada Pinkett Smith & Will Smith) but also Spike Lee and others.

Images given

Are there enough positive images on the UK's screen in soaps, the news and films? What are black characters portrayed as? Do the black actors have a say in the roles they are given? Do they have the freedom to decline a role? If a negative stereotype will be portrayed and will they get work after?

Celebrities can be torn down easily even with false accusations by the time the truth is revealed the damage has already been done to their reputation costing them their career or future earnings. So as easy as they can be brought to the limelight they can be torn down, which helps to sell magazines, newspapers and get more viewers which in turn generates higher advertising revenue.

Often in rap music there are perceived gangsters or criminals saying how they used to make money illegally by selling drugs but our youth have to ask themselves did the celebrity genuinely do this and even if they did are they themselves in the same situation that warrants illegal activity. Looking towards the future how sustainable is this activity? There is normally only one consequence and that is jail there is no future in it.

An article "the opportunity agenda" states media images have the greatest impact on perceptions of black people, when viewers have less real world experience they rely on the media world. Stereotypical images portrayed often get related to black people and this can cause issues in society with:

- people considering black people more violent

- Not trusting

- Being considered more likely to be involved with drugs

- Lack of sympathy or identification with black people

Negative media stereotypes can lead to low self-esteem and reduced expectations.

The reasons given for a lack of black people represented in the media or represented positively is:

- The producer-may be going by his own bias view

- Lack of television stations, producers and editors that are black

- Producers and writers may be considering what they perceive the audience wants to   see or will respond to

- Political pressures

Portrayal of Black people

Black males tend to be portrayed as criminals or aggressive in some form.

If we look at computer games there is a lack of black positive main characters and just like in life on TV they are given background roles, they are not linked to luxury good items in adverts nor experts when opinion is sought on a subject in the news.

When black males are represented they tend not to be represented as father figures that are positive.

To sum up the media portrayal of black males they are represented with little range and as being physical in sports or having entertainment abilities.

Naturally like any race there are people that are bad and that may give a bad image of their race but people have to keep this in mind and not use a few people's actions to label all.

One obvious solution to get more representation of black people to be more positive and represented is to have more black people throughout the media in all forms from behind the camera as a cameraman, producer to acting and more.

There has been a recent spate of killings of black men and women by police and whether there are more or the coverage is more due to social media it seems when a black person is killed the justification by the media is always to look for previous convictions or associations like being a member of the black panthers to justify the killing whereas when white killers mass kill their mental health is used or they are referred to as a loner. This has led to the blacklivesmatter movement which tries to highlight the issue of injustice by police towards black people and even at court level when the judge does not give a sentence to the officer for the killing committed.

In terms of media there is the old fashioned form of TV, news, newspapers and radio which often required users to firstly purchase or look for this form of media but with social media our children are being reached faster than ever with children following celebrities activities through snapchat, Facebook, twitter or instagram. Often they do not necessarily need to follow someone but merely have a friend that shares an interest in something and then it becomes viewable to that child.

Who is teaching and influencing our children? If the answer is not you and your family then it will be friends and the media which means they can learn very different lifestyles to that which they grow up in. There have been people from rich backgrounds who portray a lifestyle where they feel they need to commit crime even though they can afford the things they thief and poor people who feel so oppressed they commit crimes believing the system is against them.

Chapter Eight

The effects of slavery

Summary

The effects of slavery can still be felt by the black race and discrimination still takes place. Open discrimination was still taking place up till the late 1960's in America so generations have still not had long to benefit from higher paid jobs from less discrimination a chance to buy property, vote and better themselves.

Introduction

Slavery

The Atlantic slave trade lasted roughly 400 years from the 1440's until the early 1800's.

The thirteenth amendment (1865) ended slavery and slave owners were paid millions if not billions after the abolition of slavery this was supposedly to compensate for the money spent on purchasing the slaves and loss of perceived income from the work they would perform but what about the slave who has been injured, raped, killed, humiliated in front of their own families at times. Black people have been told to forget about it with no reparations even the Native Americans in America do not pay tax and now have casinos.

During peaceful times in Africa it was hard to get slaves but during war gold was needed and captured enemies were traded as slaves. It was mostly men taken to be used as slaves in America it is thought two thirds were male one third female but estimated 12m Africans. The loss of the strongest men in Ghana is argued as being a reason for its lack of development. Some would argue Africans had slaves themselves and thus in some way are to blame but these slaves were from internal rivalries and not treated in the same manner as they were later used for, although they were slaves in Africa they could still marry the slave owners family and had rights and were paid.

Black slaves were important as labourers in the plantation in Brazil, the Caribbean and North/South parts of America. The slave trade effected the British economy in the 18th century with British cotton mills depending on slave produced cotton, sugar and tobacco. Weapons trade from Europe kept divisions in Africa and increased political instability in West-Africa.

The slave trade also meant there were less able-bodied men making it easy for European's to colonise and whilst slowing the African population growth, African societies had such a low population density their ability to trade world-wide was limited. Engaging in other activities and building cities was also affected.

Colonialism

Whilst addressing slavery colonialism should also be mentioned the country in charge of the colonised country often limited colonial trade so that all imports and exports were to or from the main country. Almost all former colonies are underdeveloped countries today. Colonialism in simplistic terms involved one country having control fully or partially over another country in terms of politics, trade and commerce whilst occupying it with settlers for the purpose of economic exploitation.

Some would argue they brought civilisation to places giving a sense of democracy or understanding of different values but many would question the need and benefit. Colonialist countries include:

-United Kingdom
-Portugal
-France
-Spain
-Russia
-Turkey
-Netherlands
-United States
-Italy
-Germany
-Japan
-Belgium
-Denmark & Norway

This list may not cover all but gives a brief overview.

The Civil Rights Movement

Even after slavery there was still enforced discrimination and segregation all over. Enforced by people, but the place we can see in history that enforced this through the law and is mentioned in this chapter of the book is America as an example, but there is also South African apartheid to consider.

In America Jim Crow laws enforced segregation in Southern United States staying in force until 1965 causing racial segregation in public facilities (toilets, cafes, buses). Conditions African Americans were inferior in their upkeep, appearance and not funded the same. To add to this bank lending practices meant loans and mortgages were unlikely to be approved for African Americans, job discrimination took place. Segregation that took place in schools was only made unconstitutional in 1954 with the case of Brown v Board of Education. It is thought by many the Jim Crow laws were overruled by the Civil Rights Act of 1964 which was signed by President Lyndon Johnson.

The Civil Rights Act 1964 went as far as outlawing discrimination in public places (private schools, hotels and restaurants). The Voting Rights Act of 1965 stopped state barriers to voting for all federal, state and local elections. It also monitored elections that had a low minority voter presence.

In terms of housing the Fair Housing Act of 1968 banned the discrimination in the sale or rental of housing giving black people forty eight years to try and catch up with other races ability to purchase and save to buy or rent property this is less than one generation considering people can now live up to seventy plus years.

The African American Civil Rights Movement is referred to by many as the period of 1954-1968.

Apartheid

Another example of lasting effects of racism can be seen in Apartheid where racial segregation had become key policies long before apartheid began. Territorial segregation began with the land act of 1913 meaning black South Africans had to live in reserves and could not be sharecroppers.

When the National party gained power in 1948 they began enforcing policies of racial segregation under legislation called apartheid. In 1950 whites were banned from marrying blacks in South Africa.

A set of land laws entitled nearly eighty per cent of the land to the white minority and non-whites had to carry documents to be in certain areas, separate public facilities were enforced and the government denied non-white persons at a national governmental level. The government forcible removed blacks from rural areas and sold the land cheaply to white farmers. In the early 1960's most leaders of a resistance were in jail or killed. One of the most well-known faces of the apartheid movement Nelson Mandela, leader of the ANC was jailed from 1963-90 which drew international attention to apartheid.

The United Nations General Assembly denounced apartheid in 1973 and after thousands of black children were killed by police using tear gas and bullets in Soweto 1976, the UN voted to impose a mandatory embargo on arms to South Africa.

Some from a Western viewpoint would argue their impact on Apartheid due to their actions against flying Delta Airlines, stopped buying Coca-Cola, and stopped supporting corporations that had an involvement in Apartheid.

After this a few laws such as the ban on sexual activity between different races were dropped but it did not go far enough and sub sequential laws did not bring about the change needed until 1994 with a new constitution and non-white majority government.

Summary

The effects of slavery can be felt mentally by many in the black race feeling anger and resentment that their ancestors had to go through the physical and mental torture. And with the white race feeling guilty or ashamed their ancestors carried out such atrocities.

The social divides amongst the rich white and poor black areas still exist today in America and many parts of the world.

Financially the black race have not been able to purchase property or even live in certain areas thus have not had the same starting point to establish themselves. The white race has had over 300 years to advance their skills, wealth and more.

There is so much more to black history but this chapter is to give a brief overview and get people engaged and looking for more information to learn for themselves.

Chapter Nine

Appropriation of culture

Summary

Many cultures are seeing there is money to be made by selling and using other cultures fashion, music, products and even mannerisms. This is being helped by the media in films, TV adverts and newspapers.

Introduction

Definition

Appropriation can be seen as a dominant culture taking advantage of a smaller culture and exploiting that culture for gain or gaining from their acceptance. Things have often been appropriated due to privilege or supremacy, making it seem acceptable when it is on one race but not where it originally came from. An example is people making fun of black people's lips being fat but then there are many races that inject their lips to get a "fuller" look or being racist towards a person because of the colour of their skin but then spending money to get a fake tan or using products to look darker.

What occurs today?

Chinese and Indian shops are selling hair (weave) traditionally used by and sold by black people in shops and market stalls. Other races have seen there is money to be made from other cultures goods where a small business cannot afford to buy in bulk and sell at a cheaper price but have to stick to ordinary retail price if not higher to make a profit and pay overheads, if you buy in bulk at a warehouse you can afford to sell much lower.

Many shops are now selling West-Indian and African vegetables cheaper than the local shops can because they have seen there is a big market for it. It is good to have cheap products and easy access but in the long run this damages the small shops and the ordinary working class man trying to sell in his shop.

Recently there have been films that have used white people to portray characters in a land where the people were typically brown or black such as films shot in Egypt in biblical times, this used to occur in the past and the excuse used was a lack of black actors but now there is no reason not to cast more realistic characters by at least getting their race more accurate.

Does the appropriation lead to people of that culture, de-valuing the culture? being stolen and trying to identify with another or just feeling like they have no culture to appreciate.

Many have argued the appropriation whilst it can be viewed as flattering or add to the original idea in some form it can make light of an oppressive history making it seem minor due to a lack of understanding and experience of that race/culture.

It may be that some genuinely have a liking for a particular culture and do want to show their love for it or interpretation such as dance being portrayed different.

Hip hop was originally a form of expression by the black youth to speak about the violence and poverty in an area but now there are people with little understanding of this lifestyle just singing lyrics that do not reflect their experiences or lifestyles.

Often there are people that seek to profit from cultures that are poorer by buying their acceptance; this allows others to do what the original race/culture may have been criticised for such as wearing braids or locks that have been known as corn-rows or cain –row and calling it other names.

Often people who are non-European feel they have to give in to situations that call for a Eurocentric standard of looks. An example may be if a black female was going to an interview with her hair naturally curly and long, she may feel the need to straighten or place her hair in a ponytail to be more accepted or thought of as more professional.

Common appropriations include:

-Music- hip-hop, rap, r & b, rock and roll and more
-Hair-corn rows, braids, afro, dreadlocks
-Dances- twerking
-Looks-fuller lips, bigger bums, tans

Many would argue whatever environment they grow up in becomes part of their culture and they either genuinely see this as their culture or just try to fit in to be accepted.

There is nothing wrong with liking a particular style or fashion but there should be respect shown towards that culture and not a flippant view that it is a "new trend" or it looks better because it is on a person of a different race.

I always see the question come up when a culture has been appropriated by many like the black culture, where are these people when real issues come up? Such as injustices in the legal system (cops shooting unarmed black males). Are they prepared to march or campaign with black people to put things right or do they just acquire the parts of a lifestyle that suit their needs.

Chapter Ten

Investing in knowledge

Summary

How many of us invest in books to improve our knowledge and aid us and I am not talking about at a college or university but at home. There are subjects such as management, investment, exercise and accounts to name a few that would be worth reading just to have an idea in general.

Introduction

"An investment in knowledge pays the best interest"- Benjamin Franklin.
Investment in knowledge is an investment in you.
What you spend your time on is what you are looking to profit from whether that is positive or negative just like an old saying you reap what you sow.

Reading is important

Reading books can never be a waste of time as long as it is based on the reader's reading age. Even if it is a fantasy book reading keeps your brain active and can generate ideas and help relax you, it also improves language and pronunciation.

Reasons to read:

-your memory improves by learning characters, places and events

-Staying mentally stimulated can delay the onset of brain diseases such as Alzheimer's and dementia

-stronger deduction skills by working out what will occur based on previous experiences

-Stress relief due to the body staying still, focused and can make you use your imagination to take your mind off stressful problems

-improved writing skills and focus

-you can add to your vocabulary

Is age a factor?

No matter what age you are there are courses in many subjects that can help you understand an area you are interested in better, why not see if an area you have always been interested in is for you. There is no harm in trying, it is better to have tried and failed than to have not tried at all. Sometimes not succeeding in areas can be better for us it can make us try harder or realise perhaps this is not the area I should be focused on. If you have the chance to look at your life when it is over and see the missed opportunities you may question was it not worth trying even if you fail just to see what the outcome would be. The optimum time to learn is whilst young when the brain is making new connections through neurons

With all the problems faced with an average salary it is hard to see how to invest or what the point is if you have things that need to be bought now but sometimes a sacrifice now is worthwhile if it will benefit you in the future.

Many may be in debt but using a loan or credit card if it can be avoided is best, however some do only get through the month using these means. An alternative option could be an overdraft. Although we are told it looks good for your credit rating if you do spend via a credit card the best option is often using your own money if possible.

In your workplace do you have a pension?
Are you part of that pension? If you are not you should consider joining.
Remember earlier I mentioned poorer people tend to spend and act on what they want now and that is the attitude of many thinking they are not sure if they will live long enough to collect a pension so they will spend the money now. When you are older what money can you rely on? Would you have taken the steps necessary to be able to not have a pension?

Even C.E.O's and wealthy people have a pension even though it is a substantially different pension they will get they know it makes sense to have as a source of income.

We should all teach our children about budgeting so they understand assets and liabilities and how to balance an account.

It is never a good idea to loan money to invest unless it is a professional business loan by a reputable company and they have run through the business plan with you and given approval. Many are unfortunately falling victim to loan sharks and they do come in the form of professional companies too.

Chapter Eleven

Influential black financial figures

Summary

There are athletes, actors/producers and musicians that are black but where are the big business owners or tycoons? Where are the Richard Branson's, Bill Gates, Warren Buffet, Donald Trump and Mike Ashley's) to influence the black youth and tell them they can own their own business and be successful in the financial world. I can only think of Levi Roots (Reggae Reggae sauce) Jamal Edwards (SB.TV) with is media website and YouTube business. Where are the black land owners, bankers and brokers? In the U.K the Church of England, Windsor's and Earls own allot of land.

Introduction

Black businesses

Studies have shown in America that black owned businesses have lower sales, employ fewer workers and have smaller payrolls than white owned businesses with lower profits and a higher closure rate. These patterns have remained the same for the last two decades.

A study by Bates 1997 showed that low levels of education, assets and parental self-employment are partly responsible for low rates of business ownership amongst black people. Past inexperience and the fact that it is known amongst the community that it is harder for black businesses to succeed may lead to reluctance amongst those considering self –employment.

There are upcoming black businesses and progress is being made but it all starts at home by teaching children to work together with family first then other black people to make a better future for ourselves, without the violence, disrespect and anger towards one another. As a black man there are so many things that can be viewed as against you but if we can work together to uplift each other than that is one less thing to worry about.

Black businesses are never well established or co-ordinated to work together so that they can buy in bulk like other businesses and afford to sell at a price people will think reasonable enough to sustain a business and help the business grow. This is where an understanding from people is needed as to why when they walk in a black owned shop the prices tend to be higher with fewer products available.

Reasons given for a lack of black owned business in many articles apart from historical issues range from a lack of wealth meaning black people have less money to invest in a business and find it hard to get a business loan. There is also a lack of experience of owning a business whereas other races may have a generational business. It is proved that children of business owners are more likely to own a business.

If we look on the area of finance there is few black financial service employees such as advisors so there is not allot of representation to offer guidance or relate to when help is needed.

Black Wall Street

However the first Wall Street was in Tulsa Oklahoma America known as one of the most successful black owned communities having over 300 black owned businesses. The area started to flourish throughout the early 1900's due to an oil boom and had thriving black businesses.

The whole town (35 square blocks) was burnt to the ground under the pretence of a riot in 1921 in which white people massacred black residents and fire fighters were kept from putting out the fire by a mob. The whole riot emanated from a white elevator operators alleged assault by a black teenager.

During this time a prominent black American physician DR. A.C. Jackson was shot to death outside his house.

After five years residents tried to rebuild but when segregation was overturned many blacks moved and shopped elsewhere so the area lost its abundance.

This goes to show what investing in your community and area can do meaning the whole area flourishes instead of just multi-million dollar companies that do not give back to the community.

Chapter Twelve

The benefits of a healthy lifestyle

Summary

We can try escaping the poverty cycle financially by gaining more knowledge and trying to improve our situation by being more positive towards one another but you can also be regarded as poor by having poor health. In this chapter I look at the everyday simple decisions we make with our health when we go to eat at home and outdoors.

Introduction

The Dalai Lama, when asked about what surprised him most about humanity answered, "Man. Because he sacrifices his health in order to make money, then sacrifices money to recuperate his health".

Keeping healthy is a lifestyle choice to eat healthy and exercise regularly, yes some of us are predisposed to our genetics that may include weight gain or inherited diseases or vulnerabilities but we should not give up we can eat healthy and exercise to get the most from our bodies.

The mental element

Often the first obstacle faced by people when going to exercise is the mental element rather than the physical. You have to be mentally disciplined to say "I am going to do this exercise however many times a week and I am going to eat healthy too" otherwise there is no point. Once you get started exercising you feel better it can help you deal with stress, get better sleep, improves circulation and can be a social activity by connecting with people or friends at the gym.

Physical exercise

When we exercise we perspire thus eliminating waste this is another way to eliminate waste which most people do not realise should be daily if not twice a day depending on how much you eat is to visit the toilet to get rid of food from the colon because it should not sit there for a long period of time. Waste built up inside the body can cause all sorts of problems.

Ask yourselves if you have a car do you often buy any petrol to put in it or put what you are told it requires i.e.-unleaded. So if we take care to ensure we have the right fuel in our car should we not be more concerned about our body and what goes into it?

Eating right

With a little bit of time such as five minutes you can look up on the internet what vegetables or herbs can do for your body. So many suffer with ailments like inflammation and aches and pains and there are herbs, fruits and vegetables that can help alleviate if not cure the problem.

Often people argue they do not like the taste of fruits or vegetables but there are ways to get around this by using a blender to give you all the benefits of the blended product.
It is also best to have a blender that uses the entire product and does not separate the skin.

Some nutritionists have claimed we should eat food separate and not mix our foods. This is because certain foods are protein and certain are more carbohydrates and take a different amount of time to be processed in the body with different levels of acids required. This does not mean only eat one more than the other there has to be a balance. What the level or percentage is will vary depending on the individual. There is not one rule that is the same for everyone. It is best to look into this area for yourself because it can be very in-depth, I have just provided a brief guide on this to give people the idea without trying to get to technical or focused on one area.

Health can mean a number of things but one indicator is staying within your BMI (body mass index).

We should only re-heat food once, when my mum used to cook before microwaves I usually did not eat straight away but when she said she was heating up the food again on the stove I knew that was the time to eat because she would not re-heat it again because that was unhealthy.

Benefits of exercise include:

-a better immune system to fight off infections

- Better circulation which helps circulate oxygenated blood
-aids digestion

-removes toxins through sweat

-less stress and anxiety

-better sexual drive

Health is not just physical with the state of our body or organs but also involves our mental health. People need mental stimulation to maintain a healthy brain. Our mental state can be affected by stress which can cause depression or other mental issues such as a breakdown.

It is important to try and reduce stress on the body possibly with exercise:

-a warm bath relaxes the muscles

-talking to people about a stressful situation can release tension

-meditation with correct breathing patterns

-Music can be uplifting

-cooking

-cleaning a room or house

-gardening

-spending time with friends

-a holiday

There are many things that can be done but above is just a few ideas.

As mentioned above positive talk can be good for you and often make us do the actions which may seem hard. So rather than talk negatively "I feel tired" talk positively "I feel energetic" this gets your mind and body set and ready.

Stress lowers the immune system. For less illness it is recommended that people eat more alkaline products than acidic. For people with skin issues such as eczema and psoriasis often food can be an issue but you should also consider what type of water you bathe or shower in because often hard water has a more drying effect on the skin. I work with a person who knows chicken causes their eczema to be worse and they still eat it because they are so accustomed to it.

Overall a balanced diet, the right amount of sleep and activity can go a long way towards keeping healthy both physically and mentally. Although there are many good fruits and foods out there as with anything to much of one thing can actually be bad for you so look into how much of particular foods you can eat.

Allot of research has suggested processed foods are responsible for causing cancer it is hard to avoid allot of it but organic raw foods does seem the way to ensue you get the most from fruit and vegetables.

All of this advice on health should be considered only by adults and after consulting a doctor and looking into the benefits for you.

Chapter Thirteen

The tax system-who benefits?

Summary

Recently it has been exposed that some rich people have been avoiding paying normal rates of tax through loopholes which many are aware exist but we assume that it is not public figures that are doing this but criminals.

Introduction

It is argued by some the way to reduce poverty is by raising income tax for high earners and compensating lower earners with benefits such as child benefits or tax credits but it is also argued this can encourage a society based on benefits that understands if they earn more they lose benefits resulting in more work for the same pay or less. This is known as the benefit trap.

Increasing the minimum wage may help some but may lead to some companies not being able to pay or employ as much staff as they usually would.

Wage growth has been slow for low average earners whereas the highly skilled have seen better rates.

Many would say zero hour contracts means people are unable to obtain things they may need such as:

- A loan,

-a mortgage,

-a car;

Because they cannot guarantee their wages week in week out.

Inflation (rise in the cost of living) although at an all-time low it may not feel that way with recent stories of food and goods sizes being reduced whilst the price remains the same. Oil prices per barrel have decreased yet at the petrol station this is not being reflected.

Corporate tax

The corporate tax system can lead to tax abuse by multinational corporations leading to countries tax system being robbed of money used for public services resulting in tax payers paying more. At the moment companies can shift profits to countries with low or zero tax rates and move losses to countries where taxes are higher. The result of these actions by companies is that developing countries miss out on vital money that can be used for roads, hospitals and education and lead to more dependence on financial aid from others. Increasing the minimum wage may help some but may lead to some companies not being able to employ as much stuff as they usually would.

People in poverty or with increasing financial issues have been argued as causing increased social problems such as crime, educational achievements being lowered and reduced physical health.

Marginal tax

It is argued by some marginal tax rates creates people unable to improve their standard of living because they develop a dependency and are better off separated from their partners with single people on £17,000 doing £100 overtime being able to take home £68 but a family person on the same amount doing the same overtime taking home £27.

For those who are going to be self-employed or starting up a business never forget to take into consideration you may have to complete a self-assessment tax form to declare all your earnings or employees payments otherwise you could be taxed heavily or even jailed for non-payment of taxes.

Much of what our taxes pay for is services of government workers and government agencies which are supposed to be for the benefit of helping people on benefits but they are often on well-paid salaries and do not realise the benefits they are receiving due to people being on benefits.

As mentioned earlier ISA's do allow you to put away a certain amount of cash per year that is tax free.

Chapter Fourteen

Your aim in life

Summary

What do you want to realistically be? There is no harm in aiming big but what do you genuinely feel you can be and have a strong desire in you to achieve?
This is not always an easy question to ask ourselves and harder to answer. Most would say rich and successful but we do need to be a bit clearer in determining exactly what that is and set goals.

Introduction

An acronym used by many to set goals is SMART that has been given different meanings but I view it as standing for:

S = Specific
M= measurable
A= achievable
R= realistic
T= time specific

Anything you want to be successful at has to be something you are passionate about because people can sense and feel that and if it is not there you may give up on the ambition.

What are the steps we need to take?

-education this can be academic or self-taught

-experience in a work place or voluntary

-apprenticeships

-training

Who do we look to?

Ask yourself who do you know that has achieved the goals you want to achieve? Can you get advice and guidance from them? Ask them what the time frame for achieving their desired goal is. Ask yourself is this a job or career? The difference is one has progression involved where you can climb up with a higher salary and possibly more responsibility the other just continues with the possibility of an annual rise but no progression.

Is the goal something you can do day after day and enjoy to the point it does not seem like work? Or is it something you dread on a Monday morning.

An Action plan

Many books have suggested making an action plan for your life setting out your goals, a time period for when this should take place and steps to achieving this with strong affirmative words and to have this visible as a daily reminder. There is not always the need to focus on one thing you can have side projects to keep busy and not be consumed by one thing. Whatever you feel is going to get you to take the correct action and if you know how you work best then this is what you need to do. For some they can wake up at night and get allot of work done for some it's first thing in the morning.

This book is not aimed at promoting social mobility for the purpose of being considered equal or accepted amongst higher classes but to empower our future generations to do better and pass on more. Whether you wish to associate with a different class of people is dependent upon you and them as to whether you are accepted for the right reasons.

If you have managed to work your way up and have money to invest the next steps to consider would be:

-real estate,

-stocks,

-and being a business owner;

I know many may question has the author got authority to give advice i.e. - has he "escaped the poverty cycle" and truthfully at this point in my life the answer is no. I have started the process of trying to buy my first home and being self-employed.

If you are reading this and can recommend it to others I may get some acknowledgement as a good author and be asked to write something else. Or if it becomes a best seller I may get more work even self-employed or through a publisher. I am just hoping it can make an important impact in people's lives where they can genuinely give credit to the book for helping them and that would be the most rewarding for me.

After reading hopefully you have some ideas that you have written down and will take action upon. And hopefully this book has benefited you to make a positive change in your life and those around you.

Thank you for taking the time to read this and hopefully it has or will help.

Chapter Fifteen
Time is an investment

Summary
What you put your time into is what you can expect to get out. Those who practice their skills in particular things go on to achieve their desired goals.

Introduction
Often we hear of musicians or sports players who have had a passion from a young age and used this to develop their current profession. As mentioned in a previous chapter this is a combination of the mind focusing on a particular goal combined with positive thoughts to produce a desired outcome.

As individuals we spend our time on entertainment and relaxation in various ways that can be counterproductive there are the positive ways such as exercising or leisure activities that we enjoy and there is the negative kind, that we can all be guilty of such as watching too much TV and films.

Interaction between family and friends

Most people to an extent take time to watch something on TV or interact with their phone but too much can lead to a disconnection in our social activity with family, friends and society. We spend our time watching millionaires in different formats (sports, music and actors) this in turn generates money for them through advertisements or interviews and interest, whilst they do what they love and in turn we are not achieving what we want but perhaps desiring the same lifestyle.

In the past before radio and television I can imagine there was more social activity between families either having to talk amongst themselves or make some form of entertainment perhaps a board game or discussions on various events. Today it is rare to see a family sitting around the table eating and discussing their daily activities, some families impose a phone ban at the table which is good for setting standards and an understanding between family members that food and family time is not with our phones but talking to each other.

I myself am guilty of watching TV but I do try restricting how much I watch and exactly what I am watching for the purpose of asking how is this benefiting me sometimes a program I watch is purely for entertainment but sometimes it is educational. However I make a point of not spending hours like I used to when I was a kid in front of the television.

Positive talk

If we spend time letting others know our goals and are clear on what we are aiming for this helps people and your sub conscience align with what you are trying to do, regardless of whether they deem it to be achievable you have to be able to convince others and yourself through positive talk and not waiver based on negative feedback. If you are receiving negative feedback then you may have to look at who you are telling your goals to and whether they have your best interest in mind or challenge them by explaining exactly what you have in mind and how you think you can achieve it.

Enjoy your life whilst you are young and free from financial burdens of life. Stop waiting to get to a specific point where you feel things will be ideal, there is no ideal point. The only point to enjoy is now. We cannot live in the past and expect a future i.e.-do not dwell on past disappointments or failures.

Sources

Bates, Timothy Mason. *Race, Self-Employment, and Upward Mobility*. Washington, D.C.: Woodrow Wilson Centre Press, 1997. Print.

Fairlie, Robert W and Bruce D Meyer. *The Effect of Immigration on Native Self-Employment*. Cambridge, MA: National Bureau of Economic Research, 2000. Print.

Kerschhagel, Marc. *Opportunity for Black Men and Boys*. New York: Opportunity Agenda, 2011. Print.

Payne, Ruby K. *A Framework for Understanding Poverty*. Highlands, Tex.: Aha! Process, 2005. Print.

Tami Luhby (Feb 18th, 2015) *whites have 12 times the wealth of blacks*, CNN: CNN.

William Hardy (2014) *Riches and misery the consequences of the Atlantic slave trade*,

(2006) *Census Bureau*, U.S:

Website

"How the tax benefit system creates a poverty trap and is destroying Britain's families", Available at: *www.mothersathomematter.co.uk* (Accessed :)

Printed in Great Britain
by Amazon